MINI MESSAGES FROM GOD 2

Linda K. Henderson

ROYSTON
Publishing

BK Royston Publishing
Jeffersonville, IN
http://www.bkroystonpublishing.com
bkroystonpublishing@gmail.com

© Copyright – 2024

All Rights Reserved. No part of this book may be reproduced, stored in a retrieval system, or transmitted by any means without the written permission of the author.

Cover Design: Elite Book Covers

ISBN-13: 978-1-963136-19-7

English Standard Version **(ESV)** - The Holy Bible, English Standard Version. ESV® Text Edition: 2016. Copyright © 2001 by Crossway Bibles, a publishing ministry of Good News Publishers.

King James Version (KJV) - Public Domain

New International Version (NIV) - Holy Bible, New International Version®, NIV® Copyright ©1973, 1978, 1984, 2011 by Biblica, Inc.® Used by permission. All rights reserved worldwide.

New King James Version (NKJV) - Scripture taken from the New King James Version®. Copyright © 1982 by Thomas Nelson. Used by permission. All rights reserved.

New Living Translation **(NLT)** *Holy Bible*, New Living Translation, copyright © 1996, 2004, 2015 by Tyndale House Foundation. Used by permission of Tyndale House Publishers, Inc., Carol Stream, Illinois 60188. All rights reserved.

Printed in the United States of America

Dedication

To my husband, Charles, who is such an inspiration to me in all situations. I thank him for his existence in my life. Without him, things would not be the same. I thank God for him and my family, in Jesus' name.

Reviews About *Mini Messages from God*

- "Compelling, hard to put down, loved the relational and conversational content." – Karen B.
- "I liked the prayers at the end; it brings everything together for me." –Donnie S. Jr.
- "Liked the way things are explained. I hadn't thought about it the way you talked about them." –B.S.
- "The Word will go forth and not come back void; it's for everyone." –Beverly S.
- "It is meant for everyone. I read it, and now my husband is reading it." –Cindy
- "You did a great job, young lady, with your book; I have enjoyed it. I read it every night before bed." –Cindy's husband

- "I liked the spaces that you left so I could put my thoughts down." –Debby
- "I bought seven of them to give to my friends and family for Christmas. I can't wait to read mine." –C.F.
- "I like your book; I'm reading it now." –Debby's husband, Bobby
- "How did you know I needed something like this?" –Tina
- "I used some of your messages to encourage someone today." –Roberta P.
- "I liked it; it was good." –Charles H.
- "I have since read your book and cannot wait for the next one. It was inspirational to me. You explained things in a way I never understood or heard before." –Crystal F.
- "I am on my second go around; I see nuggets I didn't see before." I celebrate

with you all and what God is doing in your life." –Donna F.

- "It was a great, wonderful job, inspirational, and interesting. It makes me want to do better and try to help others. I want people to see Jesus in me." –Helen C.
- "I love how you explained the order in which you pray, to the Father, in the name of Jesus by the Holy Spirit." –Marilyn B.

Acknowledgements

To all of God's children who read, supported, encouraged, and gave me feedback on *Mini Messages from God*, I thank you all for taking the time to be involved in this endeavor, which has meant the world to me. I want to acknowledge all of you and thank you for the reviews you offered me, often in the very nick of time. As I finished this book, these reviews reminded me of Mini Messages from God. There were so many other blessings in those reviews that I would have to write another book. Hmmm! I want everyone to know how much I appreciate your input and encouragement. I thank God for all of you. God Bless.

Table of Contents

Dedication	iii
Reviews About Mini Messages from God	iv
Acknowledgements	viii
Introduction	xi
MAKE EVERY EFFORT	1
GREATER THAN (>)	7
AN IMITATION	13
PLEASE DON'T GO	19
COUNT THE COST	25
THIS IS THE DAY	31
SENIORS ARE	37
RESOLUTION	41
HE PAID THE PRICE	47
IN BONDAGE	53
ABC's OF SERVICE	59

ATTITUDE	63
DEAF	69
FORGET THE PAST	75
PUT YOUR ARMOR ON	81
STAY IN YOUR LANE	87
BURNING BRIDGES	93
BUILDING BRIDGES	99
HUMILITY	105
SMALL FOXES	111
A FREE GIFT	117
IT IS A PROCESS	123
REGARDLESS	129
EXPEDITIOUSLY LORD!	135
OPTIMUM RESULTS	141
About the Author	147

Introduction

Hello, here we go again. *Mini Messages from God 2* is a continuation of the original *Mini Messages from God*. I had such a wonderful response from an audience that I was not sure would be there. I believe what I said was simple enough that even a child could understand. You guys turned up and turned out in a grand fashion for me. You came to hear the Word and the application thereof. God can and will do anything according to His will. Don't pray amiss. I thank God for the plan He has shown me and the vision that has been written. Thanks for your curiosity in Christ.

God Bless!

Make Every Effort

2 Timothy 4: 21

"Do your best to come before winter."

The Bible says when trouble comes (not if it will come, not that because you are Christian, you will not have trouble), but *when* trouble comes, Paul tells Timothy, "Do your diligence to come before winter." Paul needed some things, and his time was short. He needed his cloak or coat before the weather became bleak and dreary. He also wanted some reading material, especially his writings. He was specific about telling Timothy to do his due diligence to come before winter because it would soon be cold and be too late.

All seasons have their beauty and usefulness. Paul wanted Timothy to be sure to come before winter arrived, as there would be no need to come If he waited too late. We've all experienced hard times in life, and we must be prepared for the undertaking ahead of that time. We must be prepared. There are actions that only you can accomplish in winter. Occasionally, it is just to wait until it is over. But we must prepare in the earlier seasons. There are spiritual seasons, and there are natural seasons. Farmers knew when to plant and when to harvest because of the seasons; equally, Paul also knew what time it was.

Noah did not wait until the last minute to build the ark. It took him 126 years to build it. No one believed him when he said flood, but there was no procrastination on his part. He knew his purpose. Know your purpose. We would like to jump right in; however, there is a time and a season for it all.

Be ready in season and out of season, the Word says. Paul needed his books, and he needed his cloak. He also instructed Timothy to bring Mark along for the ministry's sake. Paul lost some friends along the way. He knew winter would be long. His work in the ministry had to continue. Even while imprisoned, facing his certain demise, he had to be ready.

Later, we discover he really needed his friend. Timothy was there for him. He read to him and stayed with him for a while. We all need friends to be there, no matter what. Friends can make our journey tolerable and take us places we need to go. They encourage us in the dismal times.

The word says to "get your house in order." Be prepared for the worst times. But have faith that it will all work together for good. Once you have paid your bills, pray, and make sure your home is winterized. Help your friends and family. You are ready to endure and persevere through the demanding times. You must be prepared to draw near to God. If you do not make it before winter, it may be too late.

Prayer: Thank You, Father, for your seasons that guide us. Thank You that we can be ready in the best and the worst of times. Help us know what we need to make it through our seasons. Thank You for friends and Your Word that gives us hope. Teach us never to hesitate to ask for Your help, in Jesus' name.

Your Reflection

Your Reflection

_____
_____
_____
_____
_____
_____
_____
_____
_____
_____
_____
_____
_____
_____
_____
_____
_____
_____
_____
_____
_____
_____
_____
_____
_____
_____
_____

Greater Than (>)

1 John 4:4 (NLT)

"You little children are from God and have overcome them. Because the one who is in you is greater than the one who is in the world."

Hello Guys! There are many things in this world that are not of God. The enemy looks around to see whom he can devour, sift as wheat, or take out. He looks for someone who can be manipulated into thinking the wrong thoughts. Ghosts, goblins, monsters, and mysteries deflect from God's word, plan, and purpose.

Guys, if you have accepted Jesus Christ as your Lord and Savior, believe it in your heart, and confess with your mouth that He is the Son of God, you are protected from the world's way. And protected from the enemies' devices, from lack of understanding. Colossians 2:15 (Paraphrase) tells of how Jesus "Made a show of the evil spirits in

Hell, put them to shame, took the keys of death and hell." Evil spirits have no authority over God's children, the ones who accepted Jesus as their Savior. No influence or control can be obtained if you know the Word. Speak the Word of God over your situations. Let the enemy know that you know who you are in Christ. "I am a child of the Most High God." Tell the enemy he has no authority over you or your household in the name of Jesus. Resist him; he must flee, then be ready with the Word for next time. Pray for those who persecute you and bless those who curse you; that is your job. Matthew 5:44 (KJV) "Vengeance is mine, sayeth the Lord." Romans 12:19 (KJV)

God is greater than (>) the world against you, and as a child of God, there is no weapon formed against you that will prosper. Saul was given an oppressive spirit as the fallen King, and only the music David played gave him relief. Yet, he would not adhere to God's instructions. It would be wise for us to be mindful of our ministries, not titles, and follow God.

Prayer: Thank You, Lord, that we know who we belong to and who we need to please. The enemy has no authority or control over our actions. God, Your will prevails. Thank You that we cannot be possessed as children of God. Thank You for the fact that only Your Word is productive in our lives. In Jesus' name, Amen. Guys, how awesome is His care for us?

Your Reflection

Your Reflection

_____
_____
_____
_____
_____
_____
_____
_____
_____
_____
_____
_____
_____
_____
_____
_____
_____
_____
_____
_____
_____
_____
_____

An Imitation

Genesis 9:13 (KJV)

"I do set my bow in the cloud, and it shall be for a token of a covenant between me and the earth."

Whenever the rainbow appears in the clouds, I will see it and remember the everlasting covenant between God and all living creatures of every kind on the earth.

The bow in the sky was a covenant made by God with humanity that the world would never be destroyed by water again. God's grace toward humanity showed forgiveness and mercy toward man's ignorance of His plan. We now have an imitation of the bow to remind people of the covenant, the promise He initiated, to show us his love and faithfulness. An abundance of confusion has ensued, the original purpose of the rainbow has been forgotten, and an imitation is being celebrated and honored. "Satan is the author of confusion" 1 Corinthians 14:33.

In Sodom and Gomorrah, the effect of the imitation was uncovered when the home that Lot chose was destroyed. The sin was rampant, and the cities surrounding the area were also destroyed. The punishment and Lot's lack of positive influence in his family wreaked havoc on all concerned. You have heard the story of Lot's wife looking back and turning into a pillar of salt. In their confusion, his children decided to imitate being wives to their father, a tragedy all around. When we try to replicate an item, it will not replace the original, the authentic article.

Lucifer decided that because of his talent, position, and beauty, he could replace God on His throne. He was subsequently thrown out of heaven with a third of the angels. There are accounts in the Bible of such imitations that we, as His people, must consider. God says He will not have us ignorant of the devices of the enemy. There are many types of imitations in the world, for example, false prophets, shoes, clothes, and purses that we desire. But the people with the real thing know the difference. The imitations may look good and fool some, but they cannot replace the real thing.

Prayer: Thank You, Father, for teaching us the difference in Your Word. Satan is the author of confusion. You, Father, play no part in that. Thank You. The rainbow is a beautiful, colorful authentication of Your promises. Thank You for understanding that we can know the truth and not accept an imitation. Thank You for wisdom and discernment of the enemy's imitations and the limitations You placed on the enemy. In Jesus' name, Amen.

Your Reflection

_____
_____
_____
_____
_____
_____
_____
_____
_____
_____
_____
_____
_____
_____
_____
_____
_____
_____
_____
_____
_____
_____
_____
_____
_____
_____
_____

Your Reflection

_____
_____
_____
_____
_____
_____
_____
_____
_____
_____
_____
_____
_____
_____
_____
_____
_____
_____
_____
_____
_____
_____
_____
_____
_____

Please Don't Go

2 Corinthians 4:17 (KJV)

"For our light afflictions, which is but for a moment, worketh for us a far more exceeding and eternal weight of glory."

No one likes trials and tribulations. The temptations come when we try to live in peace and rest in God. When we strive to be happy without a care in the world, we know that while in this world, it is impossible not to be affected. It does not matter how much gospel music we listen to or how many preachers we keep as staples in our arsenal. The Word calls them trials, tribulations, temptations, and light afflictions. They are significant for us. But to Jesus, His load is easy, and His burdens are light, and these are what He has gifted us. He went to the cross in place of us. When trouble comes, He is present. So, we need not go out disturbed and confused as if no one came for us. Jesus died on the cross for us, and we cannot go out like this. Please do not go! No negativity.

We miss out on our spiritual blessings and the growing pains that come with them. We forget who we are in Christ, who we are to Him, and what He has done for us. What the enemy intends for our evil, God means for our good. Our faith is increased through pain. That is the plan and the purpose of God. We cannot go out like this, with lack and without recalling the promises God made. We see other's weaknesses clearly but cannot see our own. Please don't go! Don't go with doubt, ignorant of the enemy's device.

As my friend and I got older, we would say, "We are not going out like this." We would talk about makeup and fashions, and now we have reached a point where we talk about aches and pains. I agreed with her. I would have to talk with God about it. Jesus came so that we could have life and have it more abundantly. With promises like that, we cannot go out as if He did not come. Please don't go with unbelief! We can't go out like this.

As His children, we must remember to examine ourselves and make sure we are in the faith. We must ask God to examine us and see if there is any wicked way in us. When we refuse to ask God, there is lack of understanding what is needed. We just cannot conceive it. We need to check out the Word and do what it says, no matter our age, whether we are the oldest or youngest. Read Psalms and witness how David approached the Lord. The precious Spirit of God will keep us or place us in the way of Christ. Please don't go out like this without Jesus.

Prayer: Father. Thank You for looking us over, checking us out, ensuring we are okay, and sending us in the way of Jesus Christ. Father, we thank You for Your Son and for Your Spirit, who has carried us thus far. We thank You, Lord, that with light afflictions, we can learn and grow because You are with us. Please do not go, in Jesus' name, Amen.

Your Reflection

_____
_____
_____
_____
_____
_____
_____
_____
_____
_____
_____
_____
_____
_____
_____
_____
_____
_____
_____
_____
_____
_____
_____
_____
_____

Your Reflection

_____
_____
_____
_____
_____
_____
_____
_____
_____
_____
_____
_____
_____
_____
_____
_____
_____
_____
_____
_____
_____
_____
_____
_____
_____

Count The Cost

Luke 14:28-29 (KJV)

"For which of you intending to build a tower, sitteth not down first, and counteth the cost? Whether he has sufficient to finish less happily after he hath laid the foundation and is not able to finish it, all that behold it begin to mock him."

It comes at a price. When we build, there is a cost, whether it is a family, business, building, or building a reputation in life for us. We pay a price when we neglect prayer or a conversation with God for direction. In Luke 12:16- 21, a rich man looked around and saw everything he had gained, and it was more than enough like an overflow. Instead of asking God what his next move should be, he decided to build a bigger barn to keep all he had for himself. He neglected to consider people with low incomes or those in need. It is a great responsibility to know God's heart concerning the gifts and talents, prosperity, and success He allows in our lives. It is an awesome responsibility. This rich man was informed that his life would be required of him that very day. Where would his riches go then? All the things we have stewardship over are important, so make it count.

In God's view, children are incredibly special to Him. When we choose to neglect or leave them, we do not take authority or control over their well-being. We cannot know whose hands they will fall into. There is an obligation attached to that child. Jesus said let the children come to me. Do not deny them access to me. Do we take them to church? Do they see us making the right move? Are we selfish and still trying to work out where we belong? Stop and count the cost.

Stand up and take seriously what God cares about. Count the cost and make responsible, sound, and wise decisions, less your neighbor makes fun of you or laughs at your attempts to raise or to build. Life is short. Tomorrow is not promised. Before we know it, the children will all be grown up. What will be their legacy? A solid foundation is what they need and will only find in Jesus Christ.

One of the saddest things I have witnessed in life is children left without a father. They are committed to someone else's care. They lose their self and lose self-confidence. They lose their sense of safety. Some fathers spend little money and even less time with them. Do you know that when babies are born, they look more like their fathers so that fathers will see the resemblance and bond with that child? Fathers count the cost before you begin to build a building or raise a child.

Prayer: Thank You, Lord, for giving us choices and telling us to choose life in all of them. Thank You that, as Your children, we know Your thoughts toward us. Help us to make the right commitment toward our children in Jesus' name. Thank You for staying with us and sharing Your will. Thank You for being our ultimate Father who will never leave or forsake us.

Your Reflection

_____
_____
_____
_____
_____
_____
_____
_____
_____
_____
_____
_____
_____
_____
_____
_____
_____
_____
_____
_____
_____
_____
_____
_____

Your Reflection

This Is the Day!

Psalm 118:24 (KJV)

This is the day which the Lord hath made; we will rejoice and be glad in it.

This is the day that the Lord has made. Let us rejoice and be glad in it. Oh Lord, save us. Oh, Lord, grant us success. Blessed is he who comes in the name of the Lord. From the House of the Lord, we bless you. Guys, we have distinct days and holidays, for example, President's Day, Groundhog Day, Thanksgiving, and Christmas Day. We have Mother's Day, Father's Day, birthdays, and Independence Day.

We love to celebrate them with cakes and balloons; we get together with friends, celebrate the 4th of July yearly, where we all gather. My family at times, hosts a White Elephant Night on Christmas Eve; it's so much fun. Another group of friends would invite us to celebrate New Year's

Day. There's food, music, visiting, and lots of catching up.

We look forward to the holidays every year and love the opportunity to get together. These days, and every day, are days that the Lord hath made; let us rejoice and be glad in every one of them. Think about your day; this Psalm is concentrated explicitly on God. It expresses greatness, gratitude, active praise, and joy. This Psalm lets us know we can ask Him to save us from all things, troubles, or tribulations. We can ask for success, prosperity with our children, relationships, success in our career choices, and businesses.

Guys, this very day, God has created for our enjoyment. He created us for His pleasure. We are special in His sight. David's praise for the day was showing appreciation every day. Whatever the situation or circumstance, David was content to praise the Lord. He believed in the promises of

God. What an awesome place to be, believing in the Lord, trusting in Him, and having faith that God was working on our behalf. This is the day we should take note of the significance of praising the Lord.

I have to say that often praising the Lord can cause problems in your life. One day, David danced and praised so hard that he came out of his clothes. He embarrassed his wife and the people watching. But because it was a great day that the Lord had made, great things happened as he brought the Arc of the Covenant back to Jerusalem. He praised the Lord no matter what. Are we able to? No matter what anyone else says, be committed to God's special provision for us. Are we able to praise the Lord on this day, whatever the circumstance? We have sons and daughters to bring back home to their senses and our God's service. This is the day to praise the Lord. It is a day that the Lord has made.

Prayer: Thank You, Father, for sending Your son Jesus to accomplish, institute, and set in place all that we need for salvation, to be saved, prosperous, and successful. Thank You for allowing us to call on You in the name of Jesus by Your Spirit. Thank You for anticipating and placing us in a large place where blessings abound. Help us always to remember your goodness toward us. Thank You for saving us, in Jesus' name. Amen

Your Reflection

Your Reflection

_____
_____
_____
_____
_____
_____
_____
_____
_____
_____
_____
_____
_____
_____
_____
_____
_____
_____
_____
_____
_____
_____
_____
_____
_____

Seniors Are!

Isaiah 46:4 (KJV)

"Even to your old age and hoary head (gray hairs). I am He, I will carry, and will bear; even will deliver you."

S - Secure in the Lord. We have been promised that God will always be with us even when our hair turns grey. (Is. 46:4)

E - Entrusted with the Word of God to tell the stories like Abraham to his children and his children's children. (Gen. 18:19)

N - Notably different as children of God. We are a peculiar people, just passing through to our real home. (1 Peter 2:9)

I - Inspirational to the generations that have and will come after us. When people look at our lives, they will glorify God. (1 Peter 2:12)

O – Observant. Always watching and adhering to, listening for the Word of God to give us the words we need in the hour we need them. (Luke 12:12)

R - Righteousness of God in Christ Jesus. Given rest even with the happenings in the world around us. (2 Cor 5:12)

S - Saved and sanctified. We're set apart unto God, part of a royal priesthood. We are the head and not the tail, above only, not beneath. We are ambassadors of Christ.

Finally, seniors are the light of the world and the salt of the earth. We represent.

Prayer: Thank You, Father, that we are commissioned and authorized by You to continue doing the service You called us to do. Thank You for the goals before us that we have yet to accomplish. Thank You that it's not too late and we will never be too old to carry out your plan. Thank You for working in us until Jesus comes, Amen.

Your Reflection

Your Reflection

Resolution

Isaiah 38:1 (KJV)

"In those days, was Hezekiah sick unto death? And Isaiah the prophet, the son of Amoz came unto him, and said unto him, this is the Lord, set thine house in order, for thou shalt die and not live."

At the end of any matter, there should be a beautiful resolution. When the encounter is over, your mission is complete. There should be a satisfying resolution at the finish. When the problem is solved, a peaceful end is achieved.

In the beginning, Hezekiah was told that he would surely die and to get his house in order. As Hezekiah prayed, God expeditiously turned the table, sent Isaiah back to him, and gave him a change in the outcome. His prayer and trust in God earned him fifteen more years to live, and God defied the laws of nature. He sent him to the sundial in his incredibly beautiful garden and made the dial go backward as proof that he would be okay. What a lovely resolution when we go to God in prayer. How satisfying it is when God steps in. Read Isaiah 38: 1- 5.

In our own lives, we have countless complications, numerous instances where we see no way of escape, no way to accomplish what we need to accomplish. There is sickness and disease, as Hezekiah experienced, or the doctors may say it does not appear promising. You may not feel so good. Other issues seem destined not to be in your favor. However, when we have a relationship with God, as Hezekiah did, and serve the Lord with our whole heart we can remind God of the work that we have done. Although we know we are not perfect and are prone to miss the mark, God honored Hezekiah with a longer life. God is willing, waiting, and watching for the call from us so that He has the opportunity to respond to us. He wants to work on us, in us, and through us. God wants to add to our status and see our continual growth in Him. Joshua commanded that the sun stand still. Consequently, he won the battle. God said He would not hearken to a man like that again. But, hey, go boldly to the throne of grace as Joshua did. Who knows what could happen?

Prayer: Thank You, Lord, for a beautiful, satisfying, and peaceful resolution to our problems when we go to You in prayer. Thank You, Father, for hearing and answering prayers when we remind You of Your Word and cast our cares on You. When we cry out, You are faithful to help, and miracles happen. We are grateful for Your love, in Jesus' name, Amen.

Your Reflection

_____
_____
_____
_____
_____
_____
_____
_____
_____
_____
_____
_____
_____
_____
_____
_____
_____
_____
_____
_____
_____
_____
_____
_____
_____

Your Reflection

_____
_____
_____
_____
_____
_____
_____
_____
_____
_____
_____
_____
_____
_____
_____
_____
_____
_____
_____
_____
_____
_____
_____
_____
_____

HE PAID THE PRICE

MATTHEW 8:20 (NKJV)

"Jesus replied, 'Foxes have holes, and birds have nests, but the Son of Man has nowhere to lay his head.'"

Jesus went from place to place, house to house, spreading His message. For the most part, Jesus had no one to wash his feet, a common courtesy He was not afforded. Jesus came as a babe but grew up both man and God. Perfectly secure in who he was and tempted with all that we are tempted with. He prayed to His Father for us and listened to His Father. Jesus accomplished His purpose and mission when He paid for our sins with the high price of His life.

Jesus prayed for us; He prayed for us to be like Him. Awesome! He healed and showed the love of God wherever He went. He instructed us to choose life in every situation, not death. He wanted us to understand who He was, the prime example of who our Father is. The love of God plays out in His son.

There are times when we feel isolated like Jesus. When we choose a different path than others and are ostracized, our friends do not get it; they do not see the growth process or the next move we need to make. There is a point where new growth must take place. We may feel like Jesus with no place of comfort, no place to seek compassion, no place to lay our heads.

Listen, Jesus paid the price for you and me. Our Redeemer, Jesus, went and preached to the inhabitants of hell; He made a shew of the enemy publicly, taking the keys of death and hell and resolving the order of things to come. Can you imagine the audience he had to deal with? We think we have a hard audience with our family members. When we try to witness to them, it is a nightmare. Imagine Jesus praying for us, knowing our Father would equip us for the very thing we need. Do not be afraid; Jesus paid the price.

The High Priestly Prayer He speaks to God concerns these three things:
1. Christ prayed that God, His Father, would glorify Him so He could glorify the Father.
2. Next, Jesus prays for the faith and courage of His close disciples.
3. Finally, He prays for those who will come to faith because of the apostles writing and teachings of what Jesus did.

Prayer: Thank You, Lord, for your prayers and for paying the price for us. Thank You for redemption. Thank You for Your sacrifice here on earth and on the cross. Thank You for Your unconditional love of us. Thank You for making a place for us and sending us Your Spirit. Thank You for the best place to lay our heads, under the shadow of Your wings. In Jesus' name, Amen.

Your Reflection

Your Reflection

In Bondage

Deuteronomy 26:6 (KJV)

"And the Egyptians entreated us, afflicted us, and laid upon us hard bondage."

This Scripture is one of many that speaks of the bondage of the Israelites. Bondage takes place throughout The Old and New Testaments. Time and time again, the Jewish people were taken into bondage for neglecting their covenant with God. Some bondservants were in bondage for doing God's will, such as Paul and Silas, and many, many more who are scattered throughout the Bible.

We cannot decide what our government will do or what other nations worldwide want to accomplish at our expense. However, we can be mindful of our actions. Our Father in Heaven is the supreme authority. Individually, while all manner of evil persists, we are to follow the will of God. We have it all written down as a reminder of our obligations in our Christian walk.

When Jesus came, we as Christians were told no more condemnation, no more guilt or shame. Jesus took our sins on the cross with Him. We had to accept Jesus, believe, and have faith in Him. The grace of God came into play with the obedience of His son Jesus.

As Christians, we must not allow others, family, friends, religions, or ideas to put us in bondage of any kind. You must not let anyone or anything hold you to old ways of thinking, behaving, talking, or living a life that is not pleasing to God.

There was a time when you could have drug me along with that way of thinking or held me in bondage by what you thought of me. That time has come and gone. It is God alone that I need to please. I strive to share my insecurities and my upbringing with God. He will not use them against me, keep me in bondage or judgment because of them. It is comforting to know that He (the great I AM) will send or give you what you need.

In 1 Chronicles, Jabez asks, "Oh, that you would bless me and enlarge my territory." I have an idea of how, when, and where, but Jesus has the exact dimensions, which are endless. Jabez's name meant 'sorrowful, borne in pain.' In his day, names meant a lot, so he had to carry the weight of that name. God found him more honorable than his brethren and granted him his prayer. Read the whole prayer; it is incredible what our Father will do for us.

We must continue to grow in Him. We cannot allow misled parenting and other teaching to keep us in bondage. We tell our children many things that may be harmful or give them names that hinder them. Jabez's name grieved him. You know, there were several names God changed to suit His purpose. Abram to Abraham, Sarai to Sara, Jacob to Israel, and Saul to Paul are a few examples.

Prayer: Father, thank You for freedom. Your will is to keep me free. Thank You for Your Son and His observance of Your will and no one else's. Thank You for making our crooked places straight. In Jesus name, Amen.

Your Reflection

_____
_____
_____
_____
_____
_____
_____
_____
_____
_____
_____
_____
_____
_____
_____
_____
_____
_____
_____
_____
_____
_____
_____
_____
_____

Your Reflection

ABC's of SERVICE

Joshua 24:15 (NIV)

"But if serving the Lord seems undesirable to you, choose for yourself this day whom you will serve, whether the gods of your ancestors served beyond the Euphrates or the gods of the Amorites, in whose land you are living. But as for me in my house? We will serve the Lord."

The Israelites continuously made a habit of leaving their God and serving idols and other gods, and evil things were allowed in. Joshua wanted to ensure they knew God was still in charge of his life. He wanted them to be in one accord. Here are the ABCs of serving the Lord.

Make yourself **AVAILABLE** TO THE LORD- To hear from God, pray, meditate, seek, ask, and knock. Know your **ABILITY** in the Lord - Don't forget your gifts and talents come from the Lord.

Reward or **AWARD** from the Lord for your faithfulness and service.

Give your **BEST** to the Lord in all you do. Wait on the Lord. Serve Him.

Trust your **BELIEF** in the Lord - Not what you see, but what you do not see.

Expect your **BEAUTY** for ashes - What the enemy means for evil, God makes it for good.

Old you **CONTRASTED** with the new you in the Lord. There is a difference between then and now.

Keep your **CONFIDENCE** in the Lord- Know that He will do what He says. He keeps promises.

Be **COURAGEOUS** in the Lord. Do not be afraid, the battle is not yours.

Prayer: Thank You, Lord, for Your words of wisdom and instructions and for allowing us to be of service. Thank You for the ABCs, which are simplistic enough for all concerned. Thanks for giving us a choice of who to serve.

Your Reflection

_____
_____
_____
_____
_____
_____
_____
_____
_____
_____
_____
_____
_____
_____
_____
_____
_____
_____
_____
_____
_____
_____
_____
_____
_____

Your Reflection

ATTITUDE

Philippians 4:11-12 (NIV)

"I am not saying this because I am in need, for I have learned to be content whatever the circumstances. I know what it is to be in need, and I know what it is to have plenty. I have learned the secret of being content in any and every situation….."

Hi guys, here we go again. I never knew how much success and prosperity depended on your attitude. For instance, an attitude of praise unto the Lord, an attitude of servitude unto the Lord, an attitude that I can do all things through Christ who strengthens me, and an attitude of contentment no matter what condition I am in is required.

We all have been in need before. We have physical and financial needs; we may need a hug, someone to love, someone in human form that we can depend on. Yet, inevitably, it is just not available. We find our contentment in the Lord. Knowing He is our provider, healer, deliverer, and way-maker, David said in Psalms 37:25, "...yet have I not seen the righteous forsaken or His seed begging bread."

Elijah had a bad spell right after a powerful victory. He needed to keep moving and came upon a woman who said she was about to cook her last meal and she and her son were going to die. That was her plan; what an attitude. He asked her for the bread first and then told her to borrow as many pots as she could. There was a famine, and all the oil had dried up. Elijah told her to pour the little oil she had into the pots, and the oil continued to flow until the famine was over. The fact that she gave him something to eat first was a miracle, yet she did. She was blessed because she put her trust in the man of God. If she had said no, her scenario may have come to pass.

When we trust God, all things are possible. Our attitude is paramount in obtaining contentment in

His Word. As we use His Word to achieve His promises, the anointing will flow like oil continuously from one to another. Our attitude of gratitude, thanksgiving, forgiving, and living a life for Christ will help us be content no matter the circumstances. On the flip side, a bad attitude will find you in want and begging for bread, not in right standing with God.

Prayer: Thank You, Father, that we inherited the right attitude from You. We are the righteousness of God in Christ Jesus. Through our adoption, we have Your blood and DNA, and as Your sons and daughters, we are growing into perfection. Help us live with an attitude of contentment In Jesus' name. Amen.

Your Reflection

_____
_____
_____
_____
_____
_____
_____
_____
_____
_____
_____
_____
_____
_____
_____
_____
_____
_____
_____
_____
_____
_____
_____
_____
_____

Your Reflection

_____
_____
_____
_____
_____
_____
_____
_____
_____
_____
_____
_____
_____
_____
_____
_____
_____
_____
_____
_____
_____
_____
_____
_____
_____
_____

DEAF

MATTHEW 11:15 (NKJV)

"He that has ears to hear, let him hear."

When Jesus spoke, He would end with this piece of advice in Matthew 11:15. You had to pay attention and listen to what he had taught in the previous scripture. If you did meditate on what he said, look at the context, and discern what he conveyed, then the mystery would not be hidden from you. The same goes for the Word today.

In Matthew, Jesus implied, "Did you hear what I just said? Did you understand?" The rulers and leaders during His time were well-educated and knew the law but did not understand what it meant. Jesus came to interpret the law and set grace in place for all who believe.

Nicodemus, a Pharisee and teacher of the Jews, was well-versed in the law and would enforce it to the letter. However, Nicodemus waited until night to ask Jesus what He meant by "you must be born again." He looked at the natural process of birth and considered the improbability of going back into his mother's womb. He could not perceive the spiritual birth. Nicodemus did not have an ear to hear. Jesus intentionally taught in parables and would explain to his disciples what he meant. Everyone will not receive the truth unless they consult the Teacher.

Once in high school, I was assigned a book to give an oral report. I may have read the first few pages of the first chapter. When I got up to speak, I started off well; I was funny, my classmates laughed, and I was settling in to enjoy the rest of the story. I liked being in front of the class and receiving positive attention. However, to my dismay and my classmate's disappointment, it ended as quickly as it began. I did not read the rest of the book and could not finish. I heard a resounding "ah" in the room. Later that night, I read the rest of the book.

I did not consider that delivering an oral book report meant I needed an understanding of the contents to pass on the experience and information. I had to first hear for myself what was going on. My teacher responded, "Maybe next time you can speak with me and plan for another day." We must be taught and receive or cultivate the message. At least Nicodemus asked; to my embarrassment, I did not.

Prayer: Thank You, Father, for understanding and teaching us to have spiritual ears to hear. Thank You, Lord, for allowing us the opportunity to try and try again. Thank You that our disappointments will help us continue growing if we read the book in Jesus' name Amen.

Your Reflection

_____
_____
_____
_____
_____
_____
_____
_____
_____
_____
_____
_____
_____
_____
_____
_____
_____
_____
_____
_____
_____
_____
_____
_____
_____
_____

Your Reflection

_____
_____
_____
_____
_____
_____
_____
_____
_____
_____
_____
_____
_____
_____
_____
_____
_____
_____
_____
_____
_____
_____
_____
_____

FORGET THE PAST!

Philippians 3:13 (KJV)

"Brethren, I count not myself to have apprehended: but this one thing I do, forgetting those things which are behind..."

Guys, many things in our past must be forgotten and forgiven. These are things to grow from. We must forget our shortcomings and the things people said we could not do. We must forget past mistakes. There have been times, we did not tell the truth when we took something that was not ours. We must forget small beginnings and embrace the future. We are limited if we cannot forget and remember that Jesus came and took all our sins, condemnation, guilt, and shame.

David was the youngest son of Jesse. He was counted out by his family and made fun of by his brothers. But he was chosen by God as the next king. Saul, the present king, was jealous of his brothers too. Jesus took our imperfections, created, molded us, and shaped us into vessels of honor, something he could count on to pass on as well. Without the forgiveness we receive from God, we would be stagnant, stuck, and living in a negative past.

The prodigal son was in disgrace. Prodigal means wasteful, reckless, extravagant. He disrespected his father and walked out on his brother as heirs to his father's fortune. He left, took his inheritance, and squandered it away; he recognized what was happening and looked up from the pigpen he found himself in. The prodigal son humbly decided to go back to his father's house. His father forgot his past behavior and forgave them all.

His father set him up for success. He received his sandals, ring, his robe, the fatted calf, and a party. His brother was upset and angry and believed he did not deserve what his father gave him. But remember, brothers, God has your goodness in mind. He has a plan for you as well. Ask God to help you forget the past and be free of jealousy. Allow yourself to stand in someone else's shoes and see their perspective. Remember, guys, if you want a celebration, just ask; do not be bitter. If you have a want or need, ask your Father; He is faithful to give it to you, in Jesus' name.

Prayer: Thank You, Lord, for forgetting and forgiving us when we need it most. Father, thank You for all the experiences that are not good, but they help us grow. Lord, help us put the past behind us and keep pressing forward to a higher calling in Jesus Christ. We humbly ask for strength and courage to forgive and forget the things that so easily beset us and hold us back. In Jesus name, Amen

Your Reflection

_____
_____
_____
_____
_____
_____
_____
_____
_____
_____
_____
_____
_____
_____
_____
_____
_____
_____
_____
_____
_____
_____
_____
_____
_____

Your Reflection

PUT YOUR ARMOR ON

Ephesians 6:11 (KJV)

"Put on the whole armour of God, that ye may be able to stand against the wiles of the devil."

I can run this race that is put before me in the name of Jesus, not in my strength but by the grace and power of God. With the armor passed down to me, I can run through a troop and jump over a wall. Whatever wall that presents itself, Psalms 8:29-36. David praised God in this Psalm for all He had done for him. The battle is not mine, but the Lords. David was grateful for his deliverance. Throughout the Psalms, David speaks of his Avenger, his Savior, the one who strengthened him. God made him strong enough to withstand the enemy—a God who fought a spiritual battle for him and taught him the words to say. David wrote most of the Psalms. God will do the same for us.

We must put on our armor—the belt of truth, know Jesus the truth, and we will be set free. There is the breastplate of righteousness, the righteousness of God in Christ Jesus. Our helmet of salvation, we have the mind of Christ to understand His words. Our feet, being shod with the preparation of the gospel of peace, stand ready to go. Spreading the news of peace that passes understanding, the gospel of peace. We take the shield of faith, mustard seed size faith will do for now, and take up our sword of the Spirit, which is the Word of God. Be careful; it cuts both ways.

Today, I choose to put my armor on to withstand the enemy's advances in the name of Jesus. You, too, should ask for His help and have faith in His grace that you will win this race and run it well. It is an individual race; you are racing against yourself. You are not compared to anyone else. You are racing to beat your own time, so take your time— not your will be done, but God's. Run with excellence, purpose, and discernment so you can stand. Jesus will train us until His return; He is still working with us.

David knew that Saul's armor would not fit him; he had to work with what God had given him. Help us, Lord, to work with what You gave us. Like David, make this slingshot and a few pebbles work for me, too.

Prayer: Thank You, Lord, for strengthening us to be unstoppable in this race. You have prepared us to pass the baton from generation to generation. We are invincible in Jesus' name. Thank You, Lord, for delivering us from all our troubles. Thanks for Your presence and patience. Thank You for the whole armor of God. Help us to forget the past, in Jesus' name, Amen.

Your Reflection

_____
_____
_____
_____
_____
_____
_____
_____
_____
_____
_____
_____
_____
_____
_____
_____
_____
_____
_____
_____
_____
_____
_____
_____
_____
_____

Your Reflection

_____
_____
_____
_____
_____
_____
_____
_____
_____
_____
_____
_____
_____
_____
_____
_____
_____
_____
_____
_____
_____
_____
_____

STAY IN YOUR LANE

1 SAMUEL 10:8 (NIV)

"...You must wait seven days until I come to tell you what you are to do."

When Saul was anointed and appointed King, there were specific duties that the king could take on. Samuel was a high priest then, and he had particular duties that he and he alone could perform. The people of Israel had decided they wanted a king like everyone else. God had been with them, provided for them, delivered them, and basically proved himself repeatedly. Cloud by day and fire by night, He was with them.

They still wanted an earthly king, and though God informed them of their fate, He allowed them to have Saul as king. However, God said do not call on me anymore; call Saul. What a sad set of circumstances. What a tough stance for our God to take.

Saul was head and shoulders above the rest, tall and impressive to behold. Unfortunately, Saul was inexperienced, and Samuel, the high priest, would come seven days later to perform the sacrifices before the battle. Okay, have you ever been in a situation where you had been instructed to do one thing, but you did another? The outcome was not good at work when you disobeyed a direct order. Have you ever been dismissed when you stepped out of your lane or duties and took over someone else's?

Saul listened to the people complain about how long Samuel was taking. They wanted to know why Saul could not do it. After all, he was the king. He looked at their sour faces and decided to do the priestly duties. He stepped over into the priestly position. We find out that he was a mere mortal with clay feet. Like some of us, he had trouble staying in his lane or following simple directions.

You are anointed in your lane and in the right position to do well. Your plan is clear; your crooked way is made straight. When you veer from your assigned position or drift out of your lane, the consequences can be dire, as in Saul's case. He was allowed to stay king if he lived, yet David was anointed king secretly.

Another person's position may seem more important or exciting. We are often put in situations that show who we are and where we are in our walk with God. We need God's wisdom and help to stay where we have been appointed. Someone else's purpose may seem more accessible or more profitable. When we step out of our position and neglect our lane, we risk losing our special place.

Prayer: Thank You, Father, that I do not have to run myself ragged, running in others' lanes, creating enemies in its wake. People are testy when you get in their lane. Saul was quite angry when he knew the people liked David more than him. Thank You, Father, for giving me my lane and helping me stick to it. In Jesus' name, Amen.

Your Reflection

Your Reflection

Burning Bridges

Galatians 5:22-23 (NIV)

"But the fruit of the Spirit is love, joy, peace, patience, kindness, goodness, faithfulness, gentleness, self-control; against such things, there is no law."

We burn bridges when we lack kindness. When pressure is applied, you will know where you stand. Kindness is out of the window. When we love one and not the other, relationships suffer. Love is the principal thing. When we disagree and lose control, our words hurt. Life and death are in the power of the tongue. A fire is lit when peace is not operating. Burning bridges requires a set of skills that have not been working for us so far. The fruit of the Spirit teaches us how to compare right from wrong. We burn bridges when we speak harshly or misbehave toward each other.

The Word says that honey is better than vinegar, and a soft-spoken word sends away wrath. Be at peace with your neighbor as best as you can. Sometimes, it is hard to operate in the fruit of the Spirit because the things of the Spirit are set apart. There is no law that applies; it is spiritual. If God be for you, who can be against you? When Judas decided he would give Jesus up for thirty pieces of silver, the love of God was not in operation.

Jesus' worst enemy is and was "mammon" or money. You cannot serve both; you love one and hate the other. Judas was the treasurer or the "purse holder" for Jesus and his disciples. His true colors were revealed when he wanted the ointment that Mary washed His feet with, apparently to sell for the poor. Jesus was much more precious than any ointment. Jesus informed Judas the poor will always be with us. Judas failed to recognize Jesus as the savior of the world. The love of money is the root of all evil but very necessary. We must put Jesus first and prioritize our other loves.

The nine fruits of the Spirit would be perfect in our baskets. A lovely, fragrant array of goodness is in your basket or arsenal. When we compare them with our first instinct, we are closer to Godliness. Applying the fruit of the Spirit to every area of our lives gives you a view of righteousness in Christ Jesus.

We all have loved ones or friends and acquaintances that we wonder why they are not with us during a significant time in our lives. God has a plan and a purpose for us all. Only He knows the reason. We cannot allow money or man to interfere with that plan, but we must cultivate our fruit in Jesus' name.

Prayer: Thank You, Father, for your many blessings, Your beloved Son, and for grace and not the law operating for us now. Thank You for the Word that is written on the tablet of our hearts. Please help us, Father, not to start a fire and burn bridges we should not. Thank You for employing wisdom in our lives. Amen

Your Reflection

Your Reflection

Building Bridges

Nehemiah 2:19 (KJV)

"But when Sanballat the Horonite, and Tobiah the servant, the Ammonite, and Geshem the Arabian, heard it, they laughed us to scorn and despised us…"

There is very intricate, detailed foundational work to accomplish for building bridges. There are blueprints, skilled engineers, and laborers. Materials must be secured; nowadays, welders and cement masonry workers must be present. Schedules and a timeline must be recorded—an estimated time frame from beginning to end because there is much work to be done.

Nehemiah was so upset about the wall of Jerusalem being in ruins, and he was dismayed when the king asked him why. When he conveyed to the king the condition of the wall, the king began to help to ensure he had whatever he needed for the project. Nehemiah started to build the wall and ran into men who would criticize his efforts. If you would notice, three men harassed them from three different places. They came out of the woodwork to hinder God's work.

Many times, when we seek to build, we are hindered. Our friends and family criticize us; sometimes, if you are important enough, the government steps in. Nehemiah was determined; he carried weapons in one hand and tools in the other. Nehemiah had sat down and counted the cost. With the king's help, he had every right to be there. So, he carried on and finished in record time, fifty-two days. The Jewish people, under his direction, accomplished the task.

Nehemiah not only built the wall but also built bridges or bridged the gap among the Jewish people. It gave them hope, knowing their God was on their side.

God instructed Noah to build an ark. God began to instruct him when, where, what to use, and how to do it. Noah warned the people about the flood that would be coming. Since it had never rained before, they paid no attention to him. They continued with everyday living, probably thinking Noah was crazy as he worked day after day for over a hundred years. They ridiculed him and his family.

When we attempt to build in our lives, there are haters and naysayers, and as with Nehemiah and Noah, if you are not strong in the Lord, then you can be persuaded to stop what you are doing and give up. We can be ghosted, unfriended, or blocked. There are many more things that will cause you to stop what you are working on. But do not stop. If it is worth it to you and will please God, make it work. Bridges are delicate and intricate; handle them with love and care.

Prayer: Thank You, Lord, for building bridges between You and Your people. Thanks for sending Your son to bridge the gaps that split us apart at the seams. Jesus is our only tool or weapon to accomplish our goals and do God's will. In Jesus' name, Amen

Your Reflection

Your Reflection

_____
_____
_____
_____
_____
_____
_____
_____
_____
_____
_____
_____
_____
_____
_____
_____
_____
_____
_____
_____
_____
_____
_____
_____

HUMILITY

John 13:34 (KJV)

"A new command I give unto you. That you love one another, as I have loved you, that ye also love one another."

Jesus in Matt. 22:37 said, "You shall love the Lord your God with all your heart, and with all your soul, and with all your mind." Matt. 22:38 says, "This is the first and greatest commandment;" and the second one is like it, "You shall love your neighbor as yourself." The new command in John 13:34 speaks of humility and love.

Lord, help us operate in humility and love, not thinking better of ourselves. Help us, Lord, to be ever learning and coming to Your knowledge, God, the truth. Lord, help us to esteem others better than ourselves. Lord, help us love our neighbor as you have loved us.

Humbly, Jesus gave himself to save us, to save our souls. Humbly, He asked His Father to forgive them; they know not what they do. Humbly, Lord, help us to come before You and ask in the name of Jesus, for what we have need of. In humility, David asked God to forgive him many times. He knew how to go boldly before God and ask for forgiveness. In humility, he obtained it.

Humbly, Joseph took on whatever task that was assigned to him. He was sold into slavery, but he was put in charge of his master's business and household. He was wrongfully thrown in prison. In his humility was put in charge of the other prisoners. They saw God operating in his life. Finally, you have heard this before; he became second in command to the Pharoah.

Once I started a new job, apparently, there were some issues of dishonesty and unfairness that I could gather. After being there for a week or so, one of the young employees told me she was glad I was working there now because she felt safe. When people look at your life, they should feel something. The Word says people should look at their lives, see their excellent work, and glorify God. Let your light shine!

In humility, serve God. With humility, walk and talk with Him. Humble yourself and pray boldly before Him as you go to the throne of grace to obtain mercy in your time of need. Humor me for a minute: what on earth do we think we can do without God? Where can we go, and why would we want to? I CANNOT THINK OF ANYTHING I CAN DO BETTER THAN GOD.

Prayer: Father, help us operate in humility and not in humiliation. They sound similar; however, there is a large chasm between the two. In Jesus' name, Amen.

Your Reflection

Your Reflection

_____
_____
_____
_____
_____
_____
_____
_____
_____
_____
_____
_____
_____
_____
_____
_____
_____
_____
_____
_____
_____
_____
_____
_____
_____
_____

SMALL FOXES

Song of Solomon 2:15-16 (KJV)
"Take us the foxes, the little foxes, that spoil the vines: for our vines have tender grapes. My beloved is mine, and I am his: he feedeth among the lilies.."

Some of these things apply to each one of us. One or all? We go to church, or we do not, and we let what we think or understand push us into the small things that take us from the will of God. The Word says to pray for those who despitefully use us and bless those who curse us. The things of God are foreign to the people of the world, and they cannot understand; it is foolishness to them.

Those of us who attend church and watch television still must learn and grow as well. Small things: Jacob made a coat for his favorite son, Joseph, and not the other brothers and sisters. He caused jealousy and hate to brew in his children.

One small thing, it seems, is that favoritism can lead to a world of problems in a family.

God loves us all the same, no matter what. We must follow His direction and receive His help through it all. We all have different gifts and talents that God has placed within us. We can discern how to work it out with God's help. Foxes are small yet cunning, fast, and furious, focused on spoiling your vine.

I know someone (maybe you do too) who would lie and manipulate to get their way and makeup scenarios that would make you responsible for their condition or situation. Usually, these are things they have gotten themselves into. The parent had chosen this child to favor and not only spoil the child but also other relationships. Many times, the small foxes feed from the bottom up. They are relentless, and before you know it, from the root up, the vine is ruined.

It looks good on the outside but rotten to the core on the inside, disconnected from the vine itself. The fruit has gone bad on the branches. I love grapes, but have you ever bitten into one that has gone bad? However, it is never too late with God. His love is unconditional; He comes to find us wherever we are. The Word says He chases us down with blessings. It is never too late to change whatever small thing in our lives that hinders us and apply the Word of God.

Prayer: Father, forgive us our small transgressions that we have allowed to come in and kill, steal, and destroy our opportunities, relationships, and prospects. The things that so easily beset us. Father, help us not allow or accept anything in our vineyard that is not Yours. Please help us recognize our shortcomings and save the tender fruit You have provided us. Help us not to be ignorant of the enemy's devices. Keep us from all evil, in Jesus' name, Amen.

Your Reflection

Your Reflection

A FREE GIFT

Romans 6:14 (KJV)

"For sin shall not have dominion over you. For ye are not under the law, but under grace."

Brothers and sisters in Christ, we have been justified by the blood of Jesus. We are in the right standing with God. We may walk in the newness of life. The sinful nature that came to us through Adam's transgression and sin reigned in the world until Jesus came. He took sin on Him and paid the price which has no more power or dominion over us. The law did not apply to the Gentiles; it was given to the Jews. In Galatians, the Word says there are no more sacrifices to be made for sin. It is over and done with. Jesus was the ultimate sacrifice. Paul said no more sacrifices can be made. No more doves, bullocks, sheep, or lambs; Jesus did it all. The law could not be kept. You could not do one and not the other. You would have to do it all. Jesus took the sting of the law away, and grace was instituted as a gift. Everyone is invited in and can participate in the grace of God. You have heard it before—the unmerited favor of God is a gift.

The Jewish people would receive Jesus but still wanted the new Christians to have their foreskin removed, and they did not understand the baptism of the Spirit of God was instituted to us and to those to come. There is wisdom in the law. We can learn from the history of the law and why it was installed, but we are not under it. The Gentiles were not allowed in till Jesus came, and then the law was substituted for grace. The gift, no more shame, guilt, and condemnation, is all under the blood of Jesus. Repent and believe that Jesus is the Son of God; make Him your Lord and Savior.

There is still a struggle against sin; though the old man is dead, we are new creations. Sin still raises its ugly head to challenge us. We are forgiven but do not continue in sin so grace will abide, the Word says, God forbid.

Prayer: Thank You, Father, for the gift of Your Son, Jesus Christ, who took away the world's sins. Thank You for Your precious Spirit, our comforter and leader, who is always with us and orders our steps in the way of Christ Jesus. Thank You, Lord, for Your mercy, goodness, and grace. In Jesus' name, Amen.

Your Reflection

Your Reflection

IT IS A PROCESS

ROMANS 5:1-3 (KJV)

"Therefore, being justified by faith, we have peace with God through our Lord Jesus Christ: By whom also we have access by faith into this grace wherein we stand, and rejoice in hope of the glory of God. And not only so, but we glory in tribulations…."

By faith, we have obtained peace, and by peace, grace is afforded us in tribulation. Tribulation works patience in us. We can wait it out because God is working it out. As we glory in tribulation and patience, the word says that trouble will come; we can wait patiently and not stress. Philippians says to be anxious and not worry about anything, but through prayer and supplication (trusting in God) with thanksgiving, wait on Him.

When we give God thanks in everything, we recognize that He is always with us. We should make our request known to God. Experience is obtained; He has done it before and delivered us, and as we hope in Him, we can be assured there will be no shame.

It is a process that we must go through, grow from, and make the transformation required. The process can be hard; some things get more accessible, and some take much longer. The Israelites traveled around Mt. Sinai for forty years, and all from the older generation never made it to the promised land. Even Moses did not go in; he let the trouble and tribulation of the people cause him to disobey. God had a purpose when he informed Moses to speak to the rock for water. Moses was so frustrated with the people that he struck the rock instead. God allowed the water to flow, but the reason for his speaking to the rock was lost. God wanted the people to see something about his character—his patience with God's people. God wanted them to know His love even though they were disobedient and complaining incessantly to and about Moses.

It is easy to go with the crowd to fit in, and things appear well. Without God's positive input, we cannot achieve our goals. Our calculations require adjustments that we cannot make on our own. A negative approximation is our way of thinking, not God's. It places us in a position of inconsistency. We should never let a man turn us from God's plan.

Guys, let us work on the process, being assured of our Father's will and His good plan for us. Let us encourage each other and be mindful of the position He has purchased for us through His Son, Jesus Christ. Value others above yourself, think highly of them, and pray for them. We should go out and proclaim the good news. Guys, let us take a good look at ourselves and follow in the way of Jesus, our steps ordered by Him.

Prayer: Thank You, Father, for the process, the way, the truth, and the life. Thank You for lighting my way so my feet are sure and well-lit in Jesus' name. Amen.

Your Reflection

Your Reflection

REGARDLESS

ESTHER 6:9 (NKJV)

"And let this apparel and horse be delivered to the hand of the king's most noble princes, that they may array the man withal whom the king delighteth to honor, and bring him on horseback through the street of the city, and proclaim before him..."

Ok, guys, regardless of what we consider right or what we believe we deserve. We will not receive unless we believe and follow God's plan. Waiting patiently comes into play, even feeling like or perceiving that the answer to your prayer was no, a big resounding NO. Our expectations in life are often opposite from our Fathers. Regardless of how hard we work or how good we have been, God's plan will supersede our expectations.

Now, Haman decided to get what he deserved, that he would manipulate the process. Haman wanted to sit upon a great horse and have a parade for himself. He tried to use someone else as a scapegoat to achieve his goal. Haman wanted to be seen and appear important. Have you ever been in that position? Our best bet is to wait on God.

Haman thought all his tricks and lies would get him the attention he desired or deserved. He planned well against Mordecai and used his ethnicity against him. Haman was a Roman, and Mordecai was a Jewish man. It seemed, however, that the more Haman went against Mordecai, the more he appeared to escape Haman's evil plan. Mordecai would receive a message to move him from harm's way. Esther was in the Palace, and Mordecai was her uncle. God sends what we need at the most opportune time, regardless. In the end, Haman was far from where he wanted to be. He ended up by order of the king to lead his arch nemesis on the horse he wanted. Haman had to announce this man's greatness as he paraded him around town.

He had to settle for giving someone else what he thought was rightfully his. Have you been there? Regardless

_____

_____ (Fill in the blank).

When God is involved in your life, you are one of His children, and anything is possible. Regardless of what others say or do or what you think you deserve, God will have His reward when He comes. Make sure your life is lined up, and you are kind to others. Your gift will be perfect for you.

Prayer: Father, thank You for Your wisdom and grace in understanding what is best for those You love. Thank You for allowing us to choose right from wrong. In Your Word, it is practically spelled out. In Jesus' name, Amen.

Your Reflection

Your Reflection

EXPEDITIOUSLY LORD!

Exodus 17:9 (NIV)

"Moses asked Joshua to go quickly and pick out men to fight because the next day, he would hold his hands up, and Joshua would win the battle. Aaron and Hur went along to help, Moses keep his hands up until the sun went down. The battle was won against Amalek."

I have often asked God to make things happen expeditiously. To suddenly allow this to come to pass. Expeditiously, Lord, the woman with the issue of blood was healed. Jesus felt her touch and power leave Him. Sometimes, we need an accelerated outcome. As a parent, I have prayed for things concerning my children and other family members. I needed them to see what our father would do for us all.

As a parent, I have had to pray for something that we apparently could afford or help take care of.

Most importantly, I needed my children to see what God will and can do on their behalf. Subsequently, I taught my children to go to God first. They still come to us sometimes but will use what they have learned: God is always with us.

So, pray suddenly, Lord, expeditiously, Lord, immediately, Father, not for my accolades or attention but so that when we need you, Lord, you will show up quickly. When life offers challenges, we need an 'expeditiously Lord' moment to remember who our source is. As parents, our source (our Father) may give us permission to be the answer, but in Jesus' name.

Quickly, Lord, let my brothers and sisters realize who their savior is, our faithful Redeemer who keeps their promises. Deliberately, Lord, help us see You act on our behalf. As Moses would lift his arms to expeditiously or to expedite his victory,

Aaron and Hurr would lift his arms for him, keeping them there until the enemy was conquered.

We believe in You, Lord, whether we see the holes in Your hands or not or touch them ourselves. Sometimes, as the world is now, we need others to see You at work in our lives. Isaiah asked God what they would say of us if our God, the Almighty God, did not rescue his people. David said if you put me down in the pit, who is going to praise you.

Prayer: Thank You, Lord, that You will defy the laws of nature for us, that You are willing to quickly come to our defense and assist and love us as Your children who sometimes get lost, in Jesus' name. Help us to accelerate and use optimum speed to ensure You are on the scene in Jesus' name. Help us to always pray in Jesus' name Amen.

Your Reflection

_____
_____
_____
_____
_____
_____
_____
_____
_____
_____
_____
_____
_____
_____
_____
_____
_____
_____
_____
_____
_____
_____
_____
_____
_____
_____

Your Reflection

OPTIMUM RESULTS

1 Corinthians 7:6 (KJV)

"But I speak this by permission and not of commandment."

In all our endeavors, we focus on achieving optimal results; our tendencies and the heart that God has given us reconcile us to getting the job done as efficiently as possible. We continuously recall and repeat our greatest victories. We sit around at gatherings and inform others of our greatness. Most outstanding achievements include writing books, memoirs, and articles to ensure our legacy is passed on. There is baseball and other sports we succeeded in. If your career is stellar enough, there are interviews and honors in a Hall of Fame. I have an uncle that may make it to the National Baseball Hall of Fame.

God approved Abraham's willingness to pass on His stories; He said He could count on him to do it. So, to achieve optimal results in most things, we must receive God's wisdom and knowledge, His way of understanding, and willingness to do it. We are under grace now, and though all is forgiven, God forbids us to continue in sin.

Paul decided not to get married in his life. He recognized that he needed to concentrate on the revelation he would receive from Jesus concerning the Gentiles. However, he realized that wherever good is, evil is always present. He was even troubled with the world's way of operating and was tempted in the same way. This was Paul's choice; he wished everyone could be like him, but understood that if we chose to be married, we would have to listen to the Word of God to obey God's plan. Paul, as Saul, spent years out of God's will. He wanted to be sure to pay attention. Paul was highly intelligent and knew his choice would be difficult but worth it.

Alfred Bennett stated. "Intelligence is the ability to take and maintain a certain direction, adapt to new situations, and have the ability to criticize one's actions." That is particularly hard to accomplish with humility, with the possibility of being wrong, recognizing it, and changing it. Criticizing one's action is looking at what you may not see or what may be obvious to others. Consider, examine, or ask God to look at your life and let you know of any wicked way you are entertaining in your life.

Prayer: Thank You, Father, that we do not have to lean to our understanding, and like Paul, we want to achieve the optimal result and, like Abraham, be willing. In Jesus' name. Amen.

Your Reflection

Your Reflection

About the Author

My name is Linda K. Henderson. My husband Charles and I celebrated our 43rd wedding anniversary in 2023. We have three daughters, five grandchildren, and two new grand puppies: Mocha, a Rottweiler, and Bently, a Pitbull. I am the associate minister at Rocky Ford MBC in Paducah, Kentucky, where Elder Gregory Williams presides as Pastor. I have enjoyed life as a published author, which has expanded my horizons. New people, places, opportunities, and experiences have enriched my life this past year.

I can be reached via email at lkhendesign@yahoo.com. My books are available at Amazon, Kindle, and other outlets where books are sold. I also keep them on hand for private purchases. I am always available for book signings, book readings, vendor events, and to deliver the Word of God. Thank You, and God bless you!

www.ingramcontent.com/pod-product-compliance
Lightning Source LLC
Chambersburg PA
CBHW070453100426
42743CB00010B/1598